Thistle Dew

Selected, Collected Poems
Volume Three:

2002 - 2007

James Howard Trott

Oak and Yew
Press
Philadelphia

2015

Thistle Dew

Selected, Collected Poems, Volume Three :

2002-2007

James Howard Trott

Copyright 2008/2015
James Howard Trott

First edition 2015

Oak and Yew Press
Philadelphia

CONTENTS

After Augustine	1
Confidence Artists	2
Divers Thoughts	2
Frozen Magnolia Again	3
Ignition Charge	3
Looking for Leonids	5
You Made Me Die	6
Night Hike	6
Ocean City	9
Patter Familias	9
Prairie Agates	10
Pure Substance	11
Stained Glass Windows (series)	12
Thanks for Blood?	17
Touched by Tide	18
A Trace in Tracks	18
Turning Dust	19
The Whistle Blows	19
Dandelion Ghosts	20
Aerial Altar	21
Bow Oar	21
Friend and Enemy	22
Half A Ghost	22
...Hope To Die	23
Into Space	23
Parts Failure	24
The Last Causeway	25
Royal Audience	26
Three Short Circuits	27
Scattered Grain	27
The Trapeze Artist (In Memory of Lynn Davis)	28
Another Squirrel Shadow	29
Winter Dress	29
Ancient Cruelty	30
Armored Car Robbery	30
The Artist-Prophet	31

Attitudes	32
The Babies in the Manger	32
Bowl of Cherry	33
The Bull Elk	34
Classification of Minerals	35
Come and Buy	36
A Prairie Dweller Considers the Mountains	37
First Hand	38
Formation of Gems	39
Forebearance	39
A Desert	40
God Drives Us	40
The Invader	41
Invocation (in three parts)	41
Marriage As Three Trees	43
Morning Numbness	45
My Gifts	45
Nemesis Doppelganger	46
Not the New Birth	46
Panning For Gold	47
The Phone Lines Are Down	48
Poem In a Dream	49
Prairie Visions	49
Rebels Against Nirvana	51
Robbed At Church	52
Sepulchre	52
Shotgun Wedding	53
The Third Hand	54
The Two Termites (a romance)	54
You Must See	55
Ace In The Hole	55
Artificial Now	56
Back On Track	57
Better Means	58
Becoming Brilliant	58
Careless Packing	59
Interpreting a Color	59
The Country	60

Deathbed With A Future	61
Defense and Prosecution	61
The Difficult Metaphor	62
Disintegration	62
Doves in the Snow	63
Evicted	64
Evening Light : French Creek	64
Even Tide: In Memoriam : Gwinn Dyrland Clapp	65
Feared Too Well	66
The Lead in Formal Dance	66
The Best Gem Hunting	67
Gone	67
Consider the Hummingbirds	68
Into the Wilderness	68
In Aid Of	69
Jeweler's Mold	69
Jesus Was Not a Gentleman	69
Last Gasp	70
Lucile Making Love	71
Magpie	71
Materialism	72
Mission	72
Meeting Sorrow in the Street	73
Mourning Cloak	73
Speaking in Parables	74
Pests	75
Psychological Profile	75
The Reflective Dyslexic	76
Reflections of Not-Yet	77
Resonance	77
Sad Songs	78
Jesus' Saliva	78
Word In Silence	80
The Speed Of Healing	82
Strands	82
Summer of the Owls	83
Thin-skinned	84
This to the Next	85

Tidy Religion	85
Wanted Poster	86
No Wasted Time	87
Position Wide Open	87
Being There	88
Bucks in Velvet	89
Calvary Is Not Over	89
No Civilian Casualties	90
Daddy	91
God-damned	91
Foolin' Fish	92
Dusk Rider	93
Fruit On Tree	93
Give It Up	94
God's Hinder Part	94
Heirs Or Artifacts	95
Ideas and Artifacts	95
Jackhammers Before Easter	96
Marking Time	97
Masonry	97
MT Stands For . . .	98
Memories May Fade	98
Missing the Train	99
The Mountain	100
Too Many Flowers (after Mother Teresa)	100
Native Grass	101
Nautical Disaster	102
One Leaf	102
Pseudomorph	103
Roadside Memorials (Montana)	103
Self-Protection	104
You Send A Boy	105
Spring Frost	105
The Sweetest Frame	106
Tower In the Fog	107
Too Much	107
Wedding Jewelry	108
Winter Roses	108

The Water Is Wide (as per Dylan)	108
Jesus' Idolatry	109
By Animadversion	110
As On A Shore	111
The Meal After the Battle	111
Blue Mountain	112
Body As Dog	113
Circularity	113
Communication	114
My Complaint	114
Cross-Grain	115
Flag In Rain	115
The Flavor of Mortality	116
Joy In This Flesh	116
The Fractile	117
Moulting Geese	117
Giving Gifts	118
Head In The Clouds	118
God At His Most Pathetic	119
High Work	119
Idiot Savant	120
In Stars And Instars	121
Keyotic	122
The Last One Kissed	123
My Lover and I	124
Magnitude	124
When First We Flew	125
Miniature Handprints	126
Mother Mountain	126
March Tree	127
Napoleon of Basketball	127
KnickKnack (Urned Income)	127
Not Quite	128
God Give Us Metaphors	128
Pace for the Race	129
Parabowl	129
Phillatitude	130
Rainbow East Rainbow West	131

Robbing Peter	132
Satellite	132
Sea Fervor	133
Sky Blue Pink	134
The Smell of Morning	135
Stone Oven	135
Style	136
Sudden Ghost	136
Sweet And Careless	137
Top Rung Poetry	137
Trees in My Front Yard	138
War of the Warnings	139
Other books by James Howard Trott	140

AFTER AUGUSTINE

"I am the food of grown men; grow, and thou shalt feed upon Me; nor shalt thou convert Me, like the food of thy flesh, into thee, but thou shalt be converted into Me."
      -- Augustine, *Confessions*, Ch 7 [x] 16

This bread and drink I do transmute
Into a substance all my own,
As thou became the hungry form
For whom your breaking would atone.

Yet when I eat and drink thyself,
Thou chang'st my substance into thine,
Which as I eagerly receive,
Receiveth me, to drink and dine.

The bread and wine, their substance 'solves
Within and feeds my solvent dust,
But eating them I 'solve in thee,
Eternal grown on drop and crust.

James Howard Trott

CONFIDENCE ARTISTS

Moses fled to escape the pyramid scheme.
Pontius washed his hands of a Ponzi artist.
Asking always -- both Pharoah and Jesus –

More from the investor than he'd resource to pay:
Bricks without straw, risk without security.
But one was a swindler and one a savior.

DIVERS THOUGHTS

Distinct barrier of mass and mystery,
The line between air and water,
Surface unbroken,
Yet broken by every dive,
Shimmers across all landscapes,
Soul or soil, water and weather.

Every one of us is a diver,
Though not all in the same pond
Or even the same sort of lake,
For they are myriad.

But risk and raw faith
Are as necessary to us
As the air we breathe,
Or the water in which we swim.

FROZEN MAGNOLIA AGAIN

If you're capable of lush pink blooms
In abundance and profusion,
But every third spring at least,
Fooled by balmy days' confusion,
You blossom rich and vulnerable
'Til snatched in jaws, you're lost --
A cold snap, stops sap, petals chap,
-- You turn brown after frost.
Then you either die in protest
Or grow patient in bad seasons --
You can only bloom where you're planted,
Bud again against all reasons.

IGNITION CHARGE

The human mind may grow humble
In the last rumble and glow
When it comes to find and learns to know
Its evolution led to this: not revolution
But the Judas kiss -- not a holiday
But tristfully paying entropy after all.

The little rise before the fall
Was no progress, deserved no prize,
No trophy or memorial to some higher

James Howard Trott

Station, but preparation for devast,
The compounding of an initial charge,
As was amassed at Alamogordo, Manhattan,

Where the best minds fattened
For the day of slaughter Jeptha's daughter.
Crawled from the depth of ancient ocean,
Condensed from planetary miasma,
Result of interstellar bang,
We return to old mother belly apace,

Stillborn again, the reigning race.
For all our defiance of the second law,
It has no flaw nor any escapes.
Who holds it in terror or bows
In awe, finds it brooks no error.
Man's mind but the triglyceride

To preen with pride his tiny pop
By which the fissured atom starts
Its chains of schisms that only stop
When all is smoke and ash again --
When mind and matter are both subdued
To all that either can produce:

A little cloud of cosmic mist --
No Judas lips left to be kissed.

LOOKING FOR LEONIDS

November comes, almost winter,
(Thanksgivings often frozen)
But this year I took an hour to stand
In shaded driveway to watch for meteorites –
Shaded from the moon whose brilliant lunacy
Interrupts so many heavenly visions.
This year the Leonids were expected spectacular,
Like a hometown team of champion caliber.
I saw a few in searchlight streaks
Coursing as fireballs, brief before burnout,
As though a pinch hitter among angels or gods
Got one or two homers. Yet they were few,
(Too few the solid hits in any game)
And too many long balls caught and cut short.
Straining my eyes against the three obscurities
Of city lights, mist, and moon,
At one moment, best of the game,
I saw a sight I'd not expected --
A strange astrophysical sight:
Luminous gray, barely seen,
But coursing majestic, though strangely silent
Across the infield of my cosmic ballgame --
High geese in their flying "V" --
Not fiery but faint;
Not solitary in spectacular spotlights,
But together and dimly plodding;
Not brief and gone, but going ever on.

James   Howard   Trott

YOU MADE ME DIE

Sitting in the observation car of the Empire Builder,
My daughter concentrated on her computer game,
Between sightings of the American scenery.
I interrupted to suggest she go and lecture a smaller girl
Who kept saying "no" to her mother.
A moment later she told me, "You made me die."
"I didn't make you die," I replied --
A lie, it suddenly struck me.
In a very real sense I did make her die.
Thank you, Lord, for the observation, the further load
Upon this weight of responsibility.
Help me to say the right "No's," Lord.
Thank you, dear, for the lecture.

NIGHT HIKE

The sun was sweet as a stolen fruit
Until the mountains gulped it down,
And darkness old as dawn of creation
Obscured the signs in all that was made.

The star sparkles stab all ways
Reminding us of light beyond
The gate through which we've gone and come,
To take a journey -- to take at least
A little walk, night hike of unknowing.

This dim-lit stranger,
Our guide and ranger
Tells us about night vision --
About the way our eyes adapt
Only slowly and by degrees,
And how we lose much we have gained
In a single incandescent flash,
Trying to see by other lights.

We walk in the dark -- pick up your feet,
He says -- one step at a time,
Deliberate but go not halting.
The stones of stumbling
Begin to become our stepping stones.

Further on we learn more about
This seeing in the dark,
He tells us to concentrate and stare
At the shadowed image of his face,
Until it suddenly disappears:
He says we will see best at night
The things we look at indirectly.

Our outward senses other than sight
Become much better in the dark.
He has us learn to listen silent,
Hold our hands like ears of deer,
Behind our own -- then backward, before.
We hear new voices always there,
Blotted out for us by daylight seeing
And by louder and nearer sounds.
Far hints we hear of mystery,
Of joy, longing, and perhaps of praise.

James Howard Trott

He leads us on a darker way,
A damp and brooding forest path --
Unfamiliar smells and sounds -- we think
Of lurking unknown things and bears.

Look for little lights, he says.
As we catch glimpses of ghosts of glimmers:
Stars' flash amidst dense trees,
And their reflections in puddles or pools;
A posted sign, crushed can, white stone,
A winking code of lightning bugs --
And then ahead some sort of shimmer.

We draw near a strange revelation,
Glowing growth on fallen tree:
Mushrooms lit with blue-green light,
Unexpected candles under bushel of night,
Glory fresh in creatures of decay.

In the last stretch of our night hike,
We know we've turned, are going home.
We feel like comrades, proud, new veterans,
Though still we sometimes catch our toes,
Or start, a moment, at fading fears.

OCEAN CITY

The swells and surges of the illimited deep
Demanded I acknowledge fate,
Until the fragile butterfly
Came rowing across their inevitability
From what impossible horizon?

PATTER FAMILIAS

My father had a way with words,
A habit, sometimes semi-conscious,
Of pattering on in dialogue
Among a crew of immigrant comedians --
Patter that I loved from Pater that
For a few years, I partly hated --
For his patter and other patterns.
But now, full circle,
I talk too much
And in familiar jokes that make
My children groan half-humorously --
And for a few years,
Each with at least a bit of bitterness --
Pattern familiar.

James Howard Trott

PRAIRIE AGATES

I walked the prairie before sunset light,
The endless prairie of infinite delight,
Searching for agates until temporary night
Blew down the wind.

Stones I found tomorrow to try
For flints to cleave, to knap, though I
Know nine of ten will make me sigh
At cracks and crumbles.

It is no longer prairie except in recall,
But though the plow uprooted all
Its plants, stone-change is small,
So I make them mine.

If sage smell and blossoms of old fauna,
Are less, what is gone was passing on
So quickly, empty burrows, stilled songs
Compared to rocks.

Though the credo states the stones aeonic,
I break and shape them, a tonic
For ennui and unease; ironic
For a moment that infinite.

For what lasts best is either momentary
And of infinite value as the agates vary
Or truly eternal. (Vain to hammer parry –
We will be shaped.)

These count no sunset soon the last,
No matter may my blows devast,

I make but chips, not dust the past –
A future still remains.

Prairie flowers will perhaps return,
Lichens and insects, none can discern
Today, replace furrows tomorrow. We learn
Thus times goes on.

The prairie remains, of infinite delight,
The place I walked today will know no night,
As I and agates claim eternity our right
By maker to be made.

PURE SUBSTANCE

Turned bowls
Knapped flints,
Well-wrought poems.

Things of pure
Substance,
Beautifully shaped.

I wish I were
A diamond cutter.

James Howard Trott

STAINED GLASS WINDOW
The Nave

Dark except for one great light
Radiant in broken color
Shining like sun through water
Out across the altar, transept, and down
To the rugged wooden thing
Hinge for every entrance.

Light is born by light-bearers
Broken in the innumerable hues
And jagged shapes
All useless each;
Together, the second entryway
For heaven's profligate profusion.

Workshop

No glass passed through his hands,
Magnificent apprentice.
He builds of stones,
By wood and nails.
Yet he, broken for us,
Scores, fractures, grinds
The brittle forms for his radiance:
Treasure in fired forms,
Cracked with the rod of dire discipline
And most lavish love,
Fingers on the finest filigree
Of diamond-purposed plan.
We are his handicraft,
Whaled and winkled each and all
Toward the display we are made to show.

Glass

Sterile sand, wind-blown on dune and shore
Melted in furnace or furor
Colored by mineral,
Blown by living breath
Into a great vessel.
Cradled from crucible
For a thin transparency,
A true medium
Crucified by the ineluctable scoring
Of diamond tip, piercing skin,
Weakness of substance,
Divided heart --
The death of the vessel
Making a new creature,

Which sent again to the furnace,
Emerges humbled, prostrate and lambent.
Every sheet has its own hue,
It's blend, made so by impurity,
And care of concomitant heat.
Each has its share of internal flaw,
Surface texture and thick variation.
Sheets are formed with textured skins,
Pebbling, ripples, starbursts, stipples.
Varieties there are no man can number,
Out of wild luxury and according to plan.

The Accidents of Pattern

The wholeness of the kingdom,
The perfection of the bride,

James Howard Trott

Without an enemy mole or scar,
Will be a perfection of the parts.
And every part, each according to plan
Is being conformed to the glazier's pattern.
The light that comes into the nave
Was brought first
Through street doors,
Was broken and assembled
In shop and empty space unsanctified
Amidst the rough scaffolds
Of unfinished workmen.
The glass pieces are formed
Against a vision and a prophecy,
A plan and an invocation
Wish-colored by hands of hope unseeing.
Selection moved beyond prediction,
More or less than fate.
Is not each piece made by awful accident?

The careful scoring goes awry
From the first tap and snap of life!
Glass is only dust, and breaks
On fissures and futilities of its own nature.
The glazier does not so much
Design as daunt, work as wreak,
Nor fit with finesse as wrestle by will
And makes each piece entirely despite itself.
For all it retains its creator's image
In colors true -- there is that alone
Remains to it on glazier's bench.
All else is resistance to diamond, abrasive and touch.
Thus each particular breakage
May be called an accident,
In that combination of resistance and surrender.

This perverse partnership of dance and battle,
Proceeds by degrees and in permutations
Nearly infinite and beyond all human reckoning.
That each of the innumerable pieces is thus formed,
And all at last made to fit together
Seems too much to name either accident or plan.

Splinters and shards

Nothing is further from the lifted mind's eye,
The vision startled by stroke of awe
Before the assembled and daylit window
As the splinters and shards that are not there.
The hell of the workroom floor,
The dustbins carried daily from the
Unfinished cathedral,
Dumped without ceremony
In the half-filled foundations
Cannot be remembered in the fullness of glory.

But on the bench and in the shop,
These are the dominant forms of glass.

Every finger, many a sole,
Has been pierced once and again
By jagged needle or spear of glass
Broken off a piece being formed to the pattern.

Shards too, broken clean away
In the necessary separation of the elect,
But perhaps in the mystery, picked up again,
And dressed and seated in higher places.

James Howard Trott

Those all but formed sad remnants, too,
Of pieces broken in rebellious despair,
In the last tender chippings
Of small excrescences
And set aside.

The shop, the bench are clogged with these,
So that apprentices, often confused
Which are refuse and which the pieces,
Which shards, and which splinters,
When they think to have discovered a system,
Find as often their wounds from pieces as shards.

Ecclesia

A piece cut and chipped and ground
Is still a poor thing, a strange fragment alone
Until it is called, gathered, and fitted,
Led and leaded into the church.
What an hilarious hotchpotch this thing,
This marvelous mystery of noteworthy nothings,

Confounded conscripts confounding the scribes,
Enormous effulgence from shatterings of sand.

Does one find wisdom in the nattering of naturals?
Ought adults grow children to learn the way to heaven?
Does alien alembic produce purest patriots?
Yes and yes and yes and yet . . .
Why would God trust his treasure
To imbeciles, thieves and scoundrels?

The window passes light in colored symphony of sight,
In overtures that boom like cannons,
Sound and softly sigh together
Purer there than boyish descants,
Shine along the choir stalls
Red and white cross the altar,
Down the aisle
Along the floor,
Trodden by our blind feet
And out the door.

THANKS FOR BLOOD?

Thankful for the blood?
No! Not thankful
For the warm, sticky,
Thick, dripping,
Clotting, coagulating,
Drying, brown-black
Crackling blood.

I would be thankful --
For the abstract
Work of salvation.
But to be thankful
For the blood --
Is hard, Lord, is hard.
To be thankful for the blood
Requires my own crucifixion.

James Howard Trott

TOUCHED BY TIDE

As long as the tide touches the shells
Be they ever so fragmented,
They shine with color, pattern and life --
But five feet from the tide mark
They are but bits of brittle bone.

A TRACE IN TRACKS

The tracks along the shore,
The footprints in the sand,
Wander invariably
Close to the ocean strand.

They follow up and down
Where the tide neaps and ebbs,
Leave but for a while
An ever-woven web.
I study the expanse,
Pattern made and soon erased,
See but the comings and goings
On shore circumference traced.

TURNING DUST

The chips and dust around my lathe
Are bowls that will not mantels grace,
The ninety percent of labor and love
That leaves behind the work I turn.

Tools there are, well-engineered
To remove that wood
Intact and whole
To be made into smaller bowls,
But engineers and production lines
Seem to me to hold small place
In quirks of quest or toil for beauty.

My chips and dust I sweep and take
To the fern and rock plot in my yard,
Where chips and fungus they include
Become good mulch and someday soil,
Perhaps to nurture serendipitous
Trees and wood for singular bowls.

THE WHISTLE BLOWS
(During a transcontinental train ride)

Inside and outside the voice winds
Wind-like around corners at every crossing,
The call of those who follow the train,

James Howard Trott

A warning to those settled in the land:
Short and long signals, loud or dimly heard,
Carrying through nights
And bleating beneath the beating sun.
It signals this double-longing
Across the rivers, echoing in the hills –
A desire to leave the fields behind,
A wish to be planted firmly among the trees –
To go, to stay:
The whistle calls to everyone and all.

DANDELION GHOSTS

A field of dead flowers:
The green grass grows
Above which hover myriad
Dandelion ghosts.

And when the wind comes
Their faded glory
Will disappear entirely –
And they will be fruitful.

AERIAL ALTAR

My sister keeps with pious hope
An aerial altar to remotest gods –
Anticipates the visit, rare, divine :
Once-a-summer humming-birds.

BOW OAR
(contra Martin Greenacre)

I'm bow, no other.
I am a starboard man --
My oar never touches port.
Stroke I see far ahead, antithesis.
I have none following, before.
My back turned and touching
The rushing unknown,
I will follow stroke's pace
Where he follows cox'n's.
I will balance on my side
Those stern and portly pulls
As willy-nilly, we all slide,
Feather, and drop together.
I can no other.
I was made bow.
And though I pull on my left,
He on his starboard,
It is I who is
First in my own right.
I am bow.

James Howard Trott

FRIEND AND ENEMY

My greatest enemy
And my best friend
Got together
With just one end --

To slay me, yes,
To torment my soul --
But at last to present
Me restored and whole.

HALF A GHOST

There is a ghost that haunts us,
Fills us up with fear and lust,
With doubt, ambition, avarice
(Others pay "in God we trust")
But ever in our place and terror
Drives the sexes into error,
Pursuing what we want the most,
Pursuing always half a ghost.

...HOPE TO DIE

You hope to die?
Is it as Paul,
The desire for greater life?
Or as Judas –
One in God's eye?
Or, cross my heart,
As He hoped to die?

INTO SPACE

The way out is a bleak hope,
An oblique coping
Exit by indirection,
Successful lurch rather than launch,
Hurtling hunched
Hunkering through
The invisible barrier,
Less falcon than harrier,
Achieving both att- and
Altitude –
And it is the same
At re-entry –
Repentery cannot be dispensed
Nor dispensed with;
We must come the long way

James Howard Trott

Directly
To do and dogmatize
Correctly,
To arrive as directed circumspectly.

PARTS FAILURE

Uncle Bob, a natural mechanic and man of imagination,
Was fearful of driving on highways.
He said he could not help thinking of
All the parts in the automobile operating
Under tremendous pressures and wear -- and flaws,
Any one of which could so easily fail -- and then
The thought of the other cars and parts --
Not to mention the drivers --
Full of multiplying chances of disaster.

I fear more than Uncle Bob –
To go to the store or post office,
To buy a gift or take a phone call.
The whole universe and its parts
Fill my imagination with visions
Of how every part could fail,
And especially how I could.

Nonetheless, I drive the highways.
Faith becomes the failure of fear.

THE LAST CAUSEWAY
(with a bow to Prufrock)

Over the last causeway, the left crossing
We barely afford, into rainbow black,
Shoved into the back of the annals of time
For those to bring to mind who for sentiment or musing
Are always choosing the most piteous tale
Of one who fails for fatal flaw, insufficient awe
And endearing incompetencies;
Who loves too much or all too innocent,
Who hesitates, or has spent too much
Too soon, burnt out at noon with only his ankles wet
Before he can get to the treacherous place,
Driven to disgrace with gas still in the tank.
Oh, I'll thank you not to turn, no mutter,
To know which side your butter is breaded upon,
It won't be long surely, or boredom purely,
Will it: consider how often we quit where things
Were trying their wings, about to get better,
Or at least more interesting. And I'm sure I will,
Though I make a point – no swilling of tea,
No stirring of spoons, and grant you this boon,
I will not admit to growing old,
Whether or not these once brought fame or sold.

James Howard Trott

ROYAL AUDIENCE

I seek an audience with the king.
I've tried all audiences beside:
Lived for peers, lived for parents,
Lived for fanes of lust and pride.

Good books, they say, by author's will
Are written for the unseen reader,
For audiences of like conviction,
Or susceptible to like-minded leader.

Every playwright, every player speaks
His lines – in conversation,
Addresses those imagined aisles
Of his own people, his own nation.

I have lived poorly, written and played
For fantastic and fickle hearts and ears.
I would these latter chapters, acts,
Perform to please who better hears.

Living thus involves some loss –
Of other applause; some hopes reversed,
But when before the king I stand,
That best audience -- I'll be rehearsed.

THREE SHORT-CIRCUITS

The mountain, the tabernacle
And the holy of holies
Were none of them expertly wired.
Who touched them
Without proper insulation
Was sure to get zapped.
It took a terrible accident –
A cosmic short upon the cross,
And skills of a licensed electrician
To put them right.

SCATTERED GRAIN
(In memory of Howard Dyrland)

Interlopers now,
Though born to it,
We spilled shovelfuls of grain,
There in the spring fallow.
Poor communication:
I on top of the tank,
You at the auger.
And though your father was dead
And mine long retired,
We felt guilty,
Looking around furtively
At the brooding mountains
And alert acres.

Both briefly boys
Deserving berating,
Translated back
At breaking the old taboo.
I was angry –
And you were practical.
'Scatter it in the ditch,'
You said,
'The birds and mice
Will appreciate it.'

THE TRAPEZE ARTIST
(In Memory of Lynn Davis)

It seems an eerie distance the tethered bar descends
From high in the dim tent; so that whoever sends
It cannot be seen. Nevertheless it comes,
Above the dear voices, encouraging though hushed,
It comes gaining momentum such that I feel rushed
For lo, I must take hold when it comes if I would fly,
From here ascend the same long arc above crowd's cry.
I fear I may not catch it or perhaps lose my grip;
Somehow fall. Only one small slip,
It seems to me, from this small perch alone
Is all it would take to drop me into fear, the unknown.
It approaches! I haven't strength to catch the bar!
But from the trapeze other hands extend,
Tattooed -- my name in each scar!

ANOTHER SQUIRREL SHADOW

This short-sighted rodent doesn't know
His journey forward is a collision,
That as he hastens he draws closer,
And inevitably will meet himself.

WINTER DRESS

The snow-clad boulders are a crazy patchwork,
Each dressed differently and peculiar in its robe.
The tailor that draws the blessed snow
Down upon the horizontal planes of these rocks,
Clothing those facets in radiant white,
Also urges it further to earth,
Leaving their verticals bare and black,
Pulling sometimes the blanket off level places, too,
And leaving them out in the cold.
The lode that lades alone knows the fashion.

The raw ruins and vestigial beginnings of buildings
Become parts of one whole, soft, finished,
Under the cover of glory.

In the depth of winter
The finch has lost his gold,
But the cardinal remains
Blood red against the snow.

James Howard Trott

ANCIENT CRUELTY

An ancient form of cruelty
From a past of pain and gore
To be fixed through the flesh,
A foot nailed to the floor.
Nailed to the floor one can only spin,
Scramble in small circles
'Round the central pin –
Central pin, central pain,
Life revolving 'round one word
Beyond ones resolving.
What cruel master, what cruel God
Would inflict such torment?
Who nailed us here,
And what for? Meant he
To leave us ever pinioned,
Ever rotating in pain?
Who commissioned it?
Is it he, prisoned there,
Likewise nailed to this poor floor,
But, oh, nailed four square!

ARMORED CAR ROBBERY
(With red, white and blue lights)

Dangling from Orion's belt,
The hovering helicopter
Hangs and hunts, insists staccato,
With searching beam

Forcing itself, demanding
Of all our consciousnesses.
Inescapable.
Nonetheless our crime statistics
Do not hover
But rise.

THE ARTIST-PROPHET

In Gabalzan 'neath Mount Erefast
A sculptor wiser than the rest
Thought long and hard about the best
Material, that his work might last.

He knew that stone broke readily,
That wood could burn and even rot;
War's convulsions come, he thought,
In cycles here quite steadily.

Bronze is good and so is brass,
He thought, except that sword and spear
Are forged therefrom. Great work, though dear
In peace, does not remain immune, alas.

So all his work, 'til he was dead
He carefully crafted of plumbium,
Certain the day would never come
When weapons of war were forged from lead.

James Howard Trott

ATTITUDES

Baditude,
Faditude,
Latitude,
Gratitude.

THE BABIES IN THE MANGER

I see the stark hypocrisy –
I'm sorry – but you know it's true.
The carols, lights and bonhommie
Are not what we have made of you.

It's rather all the anxious pain,
The fear of failure, hope of gain,
The lists and taxes, trampling o'er,
The wary rush, the traffic's roar.

And when they ask where is the child?
It's not the suffering servant mild,
But rather all the voices crying,
Dogs in mangers, helpless lying.

We're the babies in the manger,
Celebrating not the stranger
Come to earth to save from sin,
But our own need, our deeds, our din.

And yet your unbelieved report
Has told us this. Rather than abort
This hopeless mission, us, unwanted,
You came yourself, then Spirit haunted

The babies in the story. We
Cry out at Christmas, set us free,
Break forth, oh barren one and sing
Bring forth your brood, high heaven's king,

Children of barren ones – many more
Than all our fertile, imagined lore
And born anew as you enter in
And scour the stables of all our sin.

Baby in the manger, father
Why endure such Christmas bother?
Why spend so much to heal the rift?
Why give such orphans so dear a gift?

BOWL OF CHERRY

The wild cherry limb that fell
    from the neighbor's yard,
Heavy with time and inclination,
Devastating our magnolia
    and laurels,
        furnished the wood.

To turn the block, a bowl blank
This Good Friday seemed proper devotion.
But faith will run, turn a metaphor, and
As soon as I started the lathe,
I saw the ghost,
The aura familiar to all turners –
Of the cherry blank's already and not yet,
The flashing-blur of the difference between
Its rough outer limits
    and its inner sphere.
Can I seriously avoid what mind
    and heart must see next,
The sharp tools, the flaying
    and falling.
And so I made a bowl that had a lot of Christ,
But on the reverse cut
    the hollowing,
The bowl broke loose and flew
And broke on the floor.
It lies there now
    and in this poem,
And in heaven.

THE BULL ELK

The bull elk
Hardy-horned harem keeper

Lofty-eyed land-seer
Is always afraid.

The battle hero
Square-jawed squaller
Clench-fisted over-the topper
Is always afraid.

The Son-of-god
Virgin-gendered Viking
Cosmos-creating all-holder
Was always afraid – yet stayed.

CLASSIFICATION OF MINERALS

The aged deposits of lake and sea
Sediments, passivity
Long and gentle, old peace portray;
While melted magmas, welded rock
With earthquake, eruption
Wrought havoc;
But luke-warm science says it supposes
Most precious stones were made
By process of metamorphosis.

COME AND BUY

> Ho, every one that thirsteth, come ye to the waters, and he that hath no money; come ye buy, and eat; yea, come buy wine and milk without money and without price. Wherefore do ye spend money for that which is not bread? and your labor for that which satisfieth not? hearken diligently unto me, and eat ye that which is good and let your soul delight itself in fatness. Isaiah 55:1-2

Free offer, free gift, for the poorest of the poor,
But to have the gift requireth more than nothing,
Something more.
Though it's offered to the thirsty,
To the hungry, without price,
Still the call is for a spending, for a kind of sacrifice.
This bread and water is for everyone
Who'd spend for that which satisfies,
Yet will fill, delight with fatness
Only he who comes and buys.

A PRAIRIE DWELLER CONSIDERS THE MOUNTAINS (Fathers Day 2004)

On fathers' day I wait for dusk
Sitting in a prairie dog village,
Watching the old men
Slip timorously from their holes
To assess this new danger among them.
The children are kept below,
Protected as well as
Timorous old men know how.

The mountains tower, another world,
An aristocracy to us prairie bourgeousie,
Motley mongrels of merchant and peasant,
Clerk and mechanic.
Working the land that owns us,
We can not lightly go to the mountains,
Not without invitation,
Not without formality,
Not without severe meditation after
Laboring long to show ourselves worthy.
They rise above us
Inspire us to our humble tasks,
And when we go among them,
It is cap in hand, quietly
And wearing our Sunday souls.
We can not stay there long,
For fear of some faux pas,
Some fatal familiarity,
Or fall into the meteoric hubris
Of considering ourselves equal.
In summer they smile, they radiate,
They abound,

But were we to approach them
Lightly in winter,
We would be destroyed.

The old prairie dogs whistle hoarsely now.
Even the mountains grow dim.
Day is father to night
Until a new generation.

FIRST HAND

The nail that pierced his right hand
Was forged of iron he had minded
Into being, into ore, into earth --
There mined by man.
The fist that drove
That same forged spike,
His image held, the hammer spanned,
Fused along the iron spike
Through iron-red blood
Met at first hand.

FORMATION OF GEMS

Everything precious is formed under fire. Not only
pure gold and Silver, molten in furnace, but sapphire,
emerald, ruby
Diamond in the depths of the earth where
The heat and pressure of mountains
Crushing utterly with the
Whole earth's weight
Refines, creates
A perfect
Gem

.

FOREBEARANCE

I could not bear for my forbears,
In greater forebearance than was theirs,
To have foreborne and thus forbarred
My bearing -- alas, for that were hard.

To be forgone, forlorn, for ever
From parents and siblings, my life dissevered!
Forbearant forbears were without merit,
For had I such, I could not bear it.

James Howard Trott

A DESERT

I am vast, stark, extreme –
A desert – expanses untold
Of which men dream
In nightmares.
She is a pool,
Limited, bounded,
Deep, mild –
In the midst of me
And all my green things
Center about her.
Without her,
I am a desert.

GOD DRIVES US

That he drives us –
yea, unmercifully,
We often are sure.
That he drives all men
admits no demurrer,
But where does he drive us
Like clouds or sea foam?
Does he drive us
to slaughter?
Or drive us home?

THE INVADER

Christ came into my camp,
Accompanied only by his holy Abishai,
Who said strike,
But he refused, had piety toward
The indiscernible image of the king in me.
He took the spear
From the ground near my head
(I kept it handy to throw at him
When ever he sang for my comfort)
And the jar of water
With which I sustained myself.

Thirsty and defenseless now,
I know myself a little
Since Christ came into my camp –
And slew me not.

INVOCATION (in three parts)

Do the breakers that rolled up Eliot's trousers
Reach our banks?
Oh, great Missouri,
You sneaking brown stream,
Glorious only to poets?

James   Howard   Trott

How can I invoke a muddied river
So near its sources,
When he needs flee abroad,
Wide as it was,
From its very mouth?

Can I claim the gods of my fathers
On the New England rocks?
His fathers' there were not enough,
And mine were but their indentured servants.

So I will pretend the modern myth,
That a butterfly's gesture on distant shore,
Moves mighty deeds – and words –
And call upon the British seas
To wet my whistle,
Fantasize a poet's drop of nectar
From Northern god's cup,
Borne back across the seas, up the Mississippi,
And home to these inland deserts
Up along Twain's rummy god
To inspire my madness.

Break English ocean, spray me, be it ever so fine,
With the dare to walk along his beach.

The Town.

The town I left was not the town I left behind,
Was not, I know what I once knew,
Is petty, paltry
Beside the town I thought it as I grew.

Beaver Passage

The beaver who built this town
Still will not use its streets.
On a placid evening he watches us,
Paddles bemused bearing willow aspergill
Along the levee looking
At what his rodent town's become.
Our pelts aren't worth much
In beads or goods,
Nor can our best teeth
Produce a gold strike,
Like the brief one that eclipsed the beaver.
He's back, and the gold gone,
Gone east with his ancestor's pelts
To enrich distant coffers and create
European and new English aristocrats,
From lineages of less endurance than his.
But his willow is for food and lodging,
Not to anoint or bless us,
Except as we remember.

MARRIAGE AS THREE TREES

Marriage is as three trees,
Fruiting in their different ways,
Offering shade or thorny boughs,
Their branches mingling as the wind soughs,
Their dappling dancing through our days.

James Howard Trott

The first tree is the tree of life,
That one from which the angels sword
Drove the ancient Bride and Groom
Into thistles, birth pangs, and gloom
Because they disobeyed their Lord.

The second is that other tree
In that same garden, alone taboo
Which she so subtly sensed as sweet.
He, poor provider, too did eat;
Then first their nakedness they knew.

The third tree stood on crossbone hill
And worser pain and purer care
Hung there in flesh transfixed by nails,
One which abides, one which fails:
Marriage's mystery consummate there.

And each to each in melded life
Is each these trees in turn and time,
Woman to man and husband to wife
Sustaining source, tempter to strife,
(And lopped to a cross) suffering sublime.

MORNING NUMBNESS

My right hand forgets its cunning,
Mumbles numbly newborn fingers,
Clutching nothing most mornings
After days firmly grasping
Hammer or trowel.
I am losing my grip.
Nonetheless and therefore,
I feel the touch of the unrelenting,
Unfailing hold of unforgetting fingers –
A matutinal momento to hands working
Daily construction on me –
Even while I sleep.

MY GIFTS

At the combined birthday party
Granddaughter Sophie, not yet two
Was designated the bearer of all gifts –
Carrying complicated crafts and intricate devices
To the delighted recipients.
She neither made nor purchased any --
As I give God's gifts to you.

James Howard Trott

NEMESIS DOPPELGANGER

We are the thing that we've feared most
-- That we most feared to be:
Incompetent, crippled, bitter, boring
--The ugly thing we've ever prayed,
We've spun up fervent spells, against –
Stares at us from our mirrors,
Paralyzes us with its dreaded glare
-- Our nemesis doppelganger.
Beware!

NOT THE NEW BIRTH

The weight and pressure of insistent hands
Upon the head and shoulders
Feels strong as the womb preparing,
The church's cervix engaging,
To deliver, to propel into ministry.
Or physicians hands,
Steadying, assisting, assuring.
But this is no sacrament,
It confers no grace;
Is but an ordinance,
No new birth but a sending.
For the church is entirely a kingdom of priests,
All sending, all sent,

Every hand and heart and head, a womb.
While birth is for life,
Sending is for a task, a servitude.
No office is a mantle,
The weight of hands no crown.
You are yet an unprofitable servant...
And a glorious son,
Yes born again, but not here.

PANNING FOR GOLD

The dedicated prospector put in long hot days,
And long frosty weeks, months and years,

Patiently working his way upstream
Along the creek where he found "color" –
Those traces, specks, bits of precious stuff
His life was built around.
He panned the gravel until the day,
That upstream spot, where there was no more.

And then he began to work up the slopes,
Seeking at last the source and vein, the mother lode.

--Which is how we ought to live I wist,
Only, in what does our panning consist?

James Howard Trott

THE PHONE LINES ARE DOWN

Across the street
And 'cross town,
The phone lines are down.

The two hands,
Those two feet,
Can't speak or meet.

They share no patter,
Make hopeless demands,
Like foreign lands.

Yet unlike, for they're one kind:
While from Babel they scatter,
They know what's the matter.

With unintelligible renown
Both desperately try to find,
The linesman of the mind.

The phone lines are down.

Thistle Dew   Poems   Volume III

POEM IN A DREAM

A dream I dreamed, a troubling dream
Of driving down a fluted stream,
A highway curve of river's flow
Upon the surface of currents so,
My burden task was writing fine
A constant ballad's watery line
Dripping at my stylus' tip
At first dictated, then slipped
Into silence as watching eyes
Bemused surmised what I could do
Without the help of words provised.
And startled I began to compose
In cadence blood-deep I suppose,
For writing those lines I briefly knew
Like the Kubla Khanist, some soma's brew,
"This is the way that we mark our time,
Writing on the blue wall of shadow."
That my couplet without rhyme,
All I recalled, or could waking know.

PRAIRIE VISIONS

I have seen a country road
Gone completely back to grass.
I have seen a railroad torn up,
It's right-of-way returned to deer.

James Howard Trott

I have seen an old house
Wearing its roof like a slouch hat
Doff that hat to the wind,
And sit down
Nearly out of sight in the weeds.

The same wind across the same prairie
Suspends the hawk as near the ground –
A harrier, he tilts and hangs
On v-shaped wings,
Viva voce, victor vanquished
Or vice versa.

The native knows a graveyard awe
Among the sticks and stones,
These bones of building,
Buildings stripped by wind and water – Seldom
by the native:
No, desecration is rare, no "using"
These worn boards and beams,
These sagging gables, slanting walls.

The heroes of these monuments
Were not unknown to our fathers,
And our fathers' fathers built beside them.
Piety trumps progress
At least a little longer.

Yet stones that once lined more ancient lodges,
Hold down these corners of fields,
Line the fencerows, heaped high --
Fifty lodges' worth in each rockpile.

A field is so much broader than a lodge,
So much more susceptible to the weather.
Thus the many lodgepoles, too, now fenceposts --
Shorter, myriad; bound with barbed wire sinew.
And yet so few the dwellings, so small the band
On these now uninhabited plains.

REBELS AGAINST NIRVANA

In our world where everyone
His own Nirvana spins,
There is little room for tragedy
Or uncanny has-beens
Who experience devastation,
Misery, broken trust –
All very un-Nirvana-like,
We note to our disgust.

James Howard Trott

ROBBED AT CHURCH

They robbed me at church again this week,
Took not just money, but my tools;
Broke in to my privacy,
My shabby vehicle.
And left me angry, confused and asking
God, why, while I served and worshipped,
Why take away instead of give?
Perhaps – because . . .
The taking is giving
Perhaps because . . .
We rob you so often
When you are at church.

SEPULCHRE

The purest breeze bearing an ethereal perfume,
Descends, and penetrates the foulest tomb,
Knows every crack, becomes a mighty wind,
Insistent, yet patiently breaking in.

Sunlight may reflect from whitewashed walls,
But the unseen current nothing forestalls,
Not plaster or brick or door sealed with stones,
Not rotten flesh or dead men's bones.

The tender tornado, the humble hurricane,
Propends toward graveyards, is profoundly profane,
Speaks sibilants to the dead, calls them with a shout,
Breaks into sepulchres, and then breaks out.

SHOTGUN WEDDING

The bride is not quite showing;
The groom seems so young;
The way they got to the altar,
Seems to many a disgrace.
Yet as the hymns are sung,
Their eyes shine.
Their vows are made to sing
As we are filled and overflow.
Each gives a ring --
And suddenly somehow I know
The Bride will be with child
At the wedding of the Lamb;
As I, the lowest of sinners,
Am knocked up by I Am.

James Howard Trott

THE THIRD HAND

When I carry lumber or drywall,
Or a few things heavier yet,
And come to gates or obstacles –
(Such combinations I've met!)
I always wish for the third hand
God so thoughtlessly didn't provide.
If I had it, I wouldn't need others,
--or Him – I've tried.

THE TWO TERMITES (A romance)

Through trials and tribulations,
They found joy and laughter,
Clasped in eachothers forelegs --
And lived happily of-a-rafter.

YOU MUST SEE

If you have not been raised as I
To see in every spark destruction,
A flood in every trickle,
Ruin in every ruction,
You will think me fickle and fussy,
Yet ultimately you must see
In every bite a fast,
In every breath your last.

ACE IN THE HOLE

When God played Satan
For poor Job's soul,
The Devil was the sucker --
His calculations, banter and boast
Were made without considering
The Holy Ghost,
God's ace in the hole.

The Spirit up Job's sleeve
Despite all his trouble,
Gave God the guts
To raise and double.
Satan was sly, counting cards, bold,
But didn't know God held the heart:

-- Down to the final card,
Job would hold.

ARTIFICIAL NOW

The artificial now we drink:
The wind that flies along our wires,
Our "aerials" suck in --
Is no now, not even artful,
But an artificial four seconds ago --
For even an artificial now is
Too dangerous to be entrusted to the public.
And if you are the only source
Of what a billion people think,
You need to cautiously control
The factory, its dispensations.
Time itself, that unwieldy river
That flows not through air,
But through everything,
Has no lag, not for a second;
Is under no control, but his
Who drank the vinegar after the wine,
Ate the grave-mold after the bread.
Nor did the powers of the air
Succeed at a now in the musty grave --
Not even for four seconds.
Living by faith is not drinking a message,
But swimming in the bold river,
And its every now is now.

BACK ON TRACK

Getting all my children
Back on track,
Wanting all the wheels
To go clackety-clack:
No side-rail, de-rail,
Turning back --
Wanting all my children
Back on track.

But maybe this old railway
With its bright steel line
Ain't all its cracked up
To be in my mind;
Maybe next station
Won't be Shang-ri-la,
Maybe these tracks
Have a fatal flaw.

Jesus help my children
And Lord help me
Find the narrow gage --
Track we can't see.
Lead us on the highway
Through the stumbling blocks.
Not to the scrap-yards,
But heaven's docks.

James Howard Trott

BETTER MEANS

Like a child who diligently studies painting,
Yet has no medium but mud;
Or my daughter learning piano
On an instrument a hundred years old
-- Impossible to keep in tune --
When we get to heaven
Our skills will be matched
By better means.

BECOMING BRILLIANT

In God we wish to shine.
His hand we trust, we say,
But trust we not yet God
On the grindingest of days. . .

Who facets will make true
That gems will brilliant shine --
Better in a crown,
Than untroubled in a mine.

And if to dust we go (dust from)
'Tis dust of diamonds
Polishes the gems
That we become.

CARELESS PACKING

On the way back from vacation
We do not bother with careful folding,
With making sure our laundry's done --
We're going home.

INTERPRETING A COLOR

The grain greens,
The rain means the greens to grow
On earth below.
Cyan and viridian
Upon this coil are signs of life
In plant and soil.
But green in sky,
A ghastly tone, makes men moan
And sickly sigh --
Like green in flesh
Where seen enmeshed disease
And death,
Decay, destruction --
So clouds turn green with hail,
Hailing ruction.
Out of heaven
Or in earth's parts,

James Howard Trott

Colors are good or bad
Depending on what's at heart.
Green may glow, in growth be zealous,
Or haughty hue of hatred jealous.

THE COUNTRY

The country where pickups are noticed as faraway
As jets -- vapor trails revealing each;
The country where the weather is known
An hour before it arrives;
Where what God made dominates
Both earth and sky;
The land of clouds and cactus blossoms;
Mountains and imagination;
Sunsets and no-see-ems;
Rolling hills and rattlesnakes;
The big and little of life;
The extremes of size, distance,
Temperature and weather;
Where nobody ever has an excuse for being bored.

DEATHBED WITH A FUTURE

Either an absurdity,
An insane disjunction,
Or miraculous hope:
Result of some unction
Not in evidence;
Not scientific,
Not susceptible to proof
According to any specific
We see, taste, measure, test.
Yet a deathbed with a future
In truth, would be best.

DEFENSE AND PROSECUTION

Attorneys two, to prosecute and defend;
Parents, a pair the rule, world without end;
Even good cop - bad cop, in interrogation,
Point to a polarity built over creation.
Not, gnostic antipathy, adversarial urges,
But a sovereign creator in whom there merges
The holiness that prosecutes,
The mercy that defends --
All the harshness and tenderness
Of worst and best friends.

James Howard Trott

THE DIFFICULT METAPHOR

The difficult metaphor
That validates life, love, and faith
In the midst of the expanse --
Of hours, of sky, of ocean/prairie/mountain
(Of the universe) --
Is worth the pursuit,
The silent stalk, the still watching.
The arrowheads and gemstones,
The moments/mementos in the stars,
Are all worth finding.

DISINTEGRATION

The tattered atom decays and casts
Its gloried electron down in the woods
To touch the mold, the moss, the stream,
To touch the inward eye,
A beam much slighter than the bits of leaf
That float and settle like a grief-worn
Heart or mind,
Although the summer's devastation
Of insect, fungi, and sap cessation
Leave a form, a paler sketch, skeleton leaf
Which falls fetched down upon the ground.

As the autumn careful cataract
Transforms atom and leaf, the fact
Is written large upon the tree
Itself now fading. Leaves in its lee,
Those thread-bare veins
Are like its boughs, clouds without rain,
A larger atom, skeleton, sketch.
It's not yet bare high on the hill
So do I dare say this world, too
Follows the course, and I a leaf --
'Till spring's remorse?

DOVES IN THE SNOW

The doves hunch themselves like good Christians,
Take up postures on the bare branches,
Best calculated to receive the least possible
Pure grace floating down from heaven,
Mourning its abundance, and the paucity of fodder.

James Howard Trott

EVICTED

Evicted -- cold heartless term --
Driven from the small apartment
You've called home.
Sent out into the unknown world,
All your possessions removed;
Placed upon the curb.
Some payment overdue, some debt built up,
The landlord can't want the place himself --
But he never claimed to be your friend
(He was far behind in repairs).
So now you're evicted and what do you know?
If you have a father who still lives and loves you,
And if He has a home – then go.

EVENING LIGHT
French Creek

The light paths open through the wood
At evening.
Now no dapples dazzle, dim or daunt
The forest haunt.
The floor of moss and mould
Our feet must hold is better lit
Than e'er it was since dawn.

And though we know these too fade,
We solemnly exult, and thank is made
In every seeing heart,
For light paths clear that lead from here
To where the light dwells, never drear;
Though soon from these 'twill fade.

EVEN TIDE
In Memoriam : Gwinn Dyrland Clapp

When evening comes caressingly on its even tide
Around these fragile houses, not by best stone denied,
It rises o'er the humblest first, the cottage of the poor,
Which stands not on hill crests that last light store.
Then all we thought of bright day at its first early
    turning
Has suffered a sea-change, more than a yaw of yearning
For another flood, another shore, another feast for bride:
Another running of the sea in the better easterly tide.
Who dwelt in the cottage goes before: our hope first
    tried.

James Howard Trott

FEARED TOO WELL

I feared him well enough -- too well
I feared him all the way to hell.
It is another shibboleth he gave,
A test of how we see the grave,
That he commands me do as he
And love the fearful enemy.
But I have hedged my bets in this
As in much else, tempered my hope
With earthly tactics enough to cope,
So that when I find my dangerous neighbor
Has died, I know I shirked my labor
For that vine -- never gone near
Because I saw him through my fear.
He is gone now -- his family tearful --
Perhaps to that eternity most fearful,
And my little love cast not out fear.
Lord, forgive me, who has never been here.

THE LEAD IN FORMAL DANCE

In formal dancing, though we say conventionally
The man leads, yet more true 'twould be
To say that neither doth control,
Initiative is loaned, and mutually sensed --
Thus in love, in faith, thus in Christ's coming hence.

THE BEST GEM HUNTING

Sometimes the best gem-hunting
Is at the close of the day,
When oblique rays falsify so little
And the flash of the bright or glint of the shiny
Do not mislead as they did before.

GONE

The River's always gone --
Don't bother looking for it.
What you see is what you've not --
Can't capture or explore it.
Gone the water, gone the days,
Gone the boats along it.
Gone the bison, bittern, bands,
Gone the sung who song it.
Every murmur, every plash,
Every voice and call,
Gone the moment when they were
("They were," so say we all).
But strange to say, I see and sing
Something like the River,
Something flowing somewhere --
Some thing ever.

James Howard Trott

CONSIDER THE HUMMINGBIRDS

Hummingbirds
Reap not but sip,
Hem not nor sew,
A-hem not but speak plain with
Wings buzzing aloud
At each flower or feeder,
Receive wholeheartedly
What God provides.

INTO THE WILDERNESS

Everyone enjoys going into the wilderness
If not the literal wilderness.

The Darwinian enjoys going
Into a wilderness of the past.
The Freudian enjoys going
Into the interior wilderness,
And the Marxist the wilderness
Of classes red in tooth and claw.

The social, legal, and yes, religious
Wildernesses fascinate others.
The scapegoat went into it primarily
To deliver his brothers.

IN AID OF

You can't plant a young tree too close to the old
-- Seedlings too close to the trunk are shaded,
And when the old one falls at last
Are most likely to be broken;
But fire logs set too far apart
Will damp down and die out.

JEWELER'S MOLD

He wants me to allow him to melt and pour
All I have and everything more:
My silver, my gems, every ounce of gold
Into the void of his jeweler's mold.
And oh, what shape it will finally be,
I cannot know and cannot see.

JESUS WAS NOT A GENTLEMAN

Jesus was no gentleman,
His associates weren't half
As respectable as you and I.
Most were riff or raff.

James   Howard   Trott

True -- Jesus was never impolite,
Practiced no discourtesy,
For anger or fear or lust did not
Rule him as you -- or me.

Yet Jesus was no gentleman,
He had no club or bank.
He fought but once -- a deadly duel --
With one of lower rank.

Jesus was not a gentleman --
He did not have to be,
For the error was never on his side,
As it is with you -- and me

LAST GASP

If the trials you own
Should make you 'umble,
Then your last gasp
Goes as a groan, not a grumble.

LUCILE MAKING LOVE
(Based on a parental reminiscence)

Locked in a Chevy coupe
Beside Lake Michigan's undivided expanse,
While the rightful owner dances outside, cajoles,
While the wind alternately gusts and caresses,
Losing all patience with your coyness, mirth,
Though somehow still remaining convinced
This girl is unique and something more --
Asks again that you unlock the door.

MAGPIE

This bird of black and white whose call
So raucous is, collecteth all
The gewgaws which he sees or finds,
Like dons, whose nests are made in minds.
Yet seen more closely in bright weather,
What first appeared distinguished feather,
Blends in rainbow yellow and blue,
As does the academic's view.
Still honor them: these birds can't fail
To reign oe'r all for longest tale.

MATERIALISM
(Against the Gnostics)

God has been a materialist --
Just like me --
Desiring substances,
Collecting things to see,
Feel, smell, hear and taste.
Such a come-down,
Such a waste,
That God, pure spirit,
All ways chaste,
Should have died
Materialistically.

MISSION

Admitting is the admission,
And the heart of our commission
Is repentance and contrition --
Toward a sinless condition.

MEETING SORROW IN THE STREET

Meeting sorrow in the street
My instinct always is to greet
Her cheerfully, escort her aside
To sup, and in brief sympathy, to bide.

But sorrow is a messenger,
A servant of some enterprise
That cannot halt for simple friends
Nor stratagems that they devise.

Sorrow's task I must respect,
Though sorrow's speed I may effect:
Bow respectful, but waylay -- no --
Sorrow has some place to go.

MOURNING CLOAK

The rusty velvet mourning cloak
First garment hung fluttering
In the airy newly opened breeze
Of the fresh closet of spring
Is gaily trimmed
In pale blue and yellow,
As fresh as the fabric is rich.
Yet this first butterfly
Emerges first because she knows

How to sleep through death,
Takes her rest the long night
Of winter's pinch,
Which does not conquer her.
She dresses thus for resurrection,
Just as she was dressed for death.

SPEAKING IN PARABLES

Though a city set upon hill cannot be hid,
And seem impregnable – like el Cid,
There needs be some hidden place within
Against the day her enemies may break in.
A figured jewel box or jointered desk ornate
Can be filled with treasures rich and rare,
But in a drawer more subtly situate
We keep most precious papers, gems most fair.
In public speech or printed volume we announce
Those things we reckon proper to the store
Of common knowledge and posterity's regard;
But choicest thoughts we publish nor pronounce --
Wrap rather, fold in cloth of metaphor;
While all but simplest say our sayings hard.

PESTS

Five days before we left Montana,
We heard the slub-slub as they killed
Prairie dogs in the pasture to the west.
Four days before we left Montana
The crop-dusters sprayed the fields
To the north for Russian wheat aphids.
Three days before we left Montana
Some driver ran over a coyote pup
Along the road to the east.
Two days before we left Montana,
Someone shot the badger
In the coulee to the south.
Tomorrow we leave Montana --
The last of the pests.

PSYCHOLOGICAL PROFILE

Matthew was a tax collector
Until the Lord Levy'd on him,
And sent him out a collector of souls.

Peter was a fishing man,
Easily baited, a Simple Simon:
The Lord turned him a fisher of men.

Nathaniel was guileless,
Until beguiled.

The Boanerges boist'rous
Until storm-tossed.

Judas was very fastidious
With the moneybag, and his own future,
Remaining faithful to himself.

THE REFLECTIVE DYSLEXIC

He cannot type with any speed,
Reversing letters without heed
Of left, of right --What either doeth
He cannot spell, -- It is the truth,
Nor looking in a mirror tell
For sure which one can taste and smell,
Or when performing and reflecting,
Which of him is worth respecting . . .
And spirals dithering in reversed thoughts
Of motives, modes and perhaps ought nots
Until thus tangled, no wise free,
He gazes on this other he,
Who hangs reversed upon a tree.

REFLECTIONS OF NOT-YET

Often in the heat of day,
The mountains show dim above the lake,
But in their reflections
Show a purity, a depth of color,
Nearly ideal.
It is an upside down image
In a not yet world.

RESONANCE

The heat enflamed between two logs
Upon our fire, we understand,
Because we see it.

But love's more like the resonance
Between two bells or taut strings
Ringing apart,

But singing to each other
And sustaining
Each other's singing.

James Howard Trott

SAD SONGS

The same necessity that made us love the
Broken-hearted love songs
Makes these listen to songs of death --
Death, damnation, destruction,
And force us to feel
The end of a downward spiral.
It must be *fin de siecle*,
And yet, those ancient folk songs
About lost loved ones also rang
With the pain of death and destruction --
Suicide and poison, ambush and murder.
Perhaps we all long to know evil
As lofty listeners, without its experience:
Especially young, to know
The completion of life gone wrong,
Without the failure and loss of control
That go with being there.

JESUS' SALIVA

When the one who was the word
When God spoke mouths into being
Made man, he made mud first --
Oh, horror to the gnostic in us!

And when, after remaking men
Out of decaying bodies and distracted minds,
He came upon a wordless one --
Able neither to receive the seed or multiply it --
He did not speak him well,
But touched his ears --
Oh, gnostic horror enough, yet not enough --
For then he spit upon his fingers
And touched the man's tongue.
Imagine for a moment,
Oh ye quivering Mannicheans,
The microbes quivering in the sacred saliva,
Who danced in worshipful joy
At the release and privilege of divine interchange
That they, least of all creatures,
Dwelling amidst the words of him who spoke
    them,
Might turn from attacking his immortal garment
And communicate with another
More thoroughly like them.
But no, the deaf and dumb
Was no more or less a man than Jesus.
It was substantial saliva the salivator used
To give words to him
Who could not otherwise
Have tongued them.

James Howard Trott

WORD IN SILENCE

Silent was the ancient realm
God's mind reigned over:
A vastness, a nothing,
All and all that God thought,
But in the first mystery of his desire
Creation brought he forth with a word.
Through the Word all things made
That were made --
Nothing made but by the Word.
And God said. . .
And it was . . .
And God said
"It is good".
Silence no more:
Waves crashed, winds moaned,
Rivers ran, beasts roared,
And the birds sang.
All said good by God,
But God's word echoed to a silence, still
Until in the second mystery of his desire,
God made -- with hands, not words,
And enlivened with his silent breath,
A creature in his image who answered,
Who spoke back words --
And expressed his own mystery of longing,
Naming animals and finding none suitable.
So God made, as he made man,
A mate meet, another mortal speaker,
Both in His image, both talking with him
And to each other -- different, yet one,
Forming one image of him.
And their words, in the third mystery,

Made them susceptible to words --
To the deceiver, who asked,
"Hath God said?"
For God had said, set in words
One prohibition, one sign and test
Of his sovereignty and their understanding:
"You shall not eat." the other act of silent mouths,
Taking in where words issue out,
This one thing, pleasant to behold, seeming good.
And Adam, the man, stood silent
As Eve, the woman, listened and replied,
Willing to talk about it, was deceived,
So both ate, and another silence descended.
They hid and were ashamed,
The opposite of speaking good.
But when God found them
And put words to them asking, reminding,
They returned words of hiding and blame --
Especially the undeceived Adam.
So God spoke curses -- It is not good,
It shall not be good.
New possibilities opened
Between Word and silence
Which continue ours today.
Hell is a silence --
And in the center of heaven, the Word.

James Howard Trott

THE SPEED OF HEALING

Life is direst learning to arise
From little deaths,
Adjusting one's heart
To the speed of healing:
The painful pace--
Not a run nor a walk,
But a wandering. . . and a waiting.

STRANDS

I found a strand, an end of string.
I thought it grand to find the thing.
I picked it up, I wound it small
Around and round to make a ball.

But long before I'd wrapped it up
Or reached the end it trailed me to,
I found another bit of string
And thought it shame if failed me to
Pick that one up and save the strand.
So wound I both in ball in hand.

Once is no pattern, so they chide.
Two events but coincide,
But when I found that third loose end,
I felt I ought this last waste mend --

Three strands tied their diverse sources
To ball in hand by heart's strings' courses.

As now the myriad strands I've found
Still gather in around each other,
For strings are often very long
And sometimes thick upon the ground.

They seldom end, though -- like a song --
They sometimes stutter or go wrong;
At times they have their threadbare patches,
Or tangled, come in starts and snatches.

Each strand your hand has ever found,
Winds to forever, round and round --
Which tells you heaven's pilgrims bring,
Beside bare soul -- a ball of string.

SUMMER OF THE OWLS

The rain has come in steady dowsings,
Abundant -- more than abundant -- greening,
Provoking the grain to its own abundance
This summer, this round of our cycle,
The stage at which we season on the plains.
The rain has come in steady dowsings,
And the owls in three sizes,
Unusual and abundant.

The wise Demetrian ghosts who bring good rain
On our good sojourn --
Three : the great horned family in the polebarn,
Field owls along the road on posts,
And burrowing owls, staring stark
On their little stilts
Beside their gophery burrows.

THIN-SKINNED

Writers of the great plains, writers of the mountains,
Are subdued, embarrassed, as awestruck as naked
Adam before a Holy God,
For it is bare skin they have to write about:
Naked prairie where each inch of soil
Is five hundred years accumulating --
Accumulated several inches about the tepee rings
Of their immediate predecessors.
While in the city all the thick skin of writers
Is richly clothed in concrete
And latest fashions.

THIS TO THE NEXT

No matter who you take for text
In this great library not yet indexed,
The theme is always from this to the next.

This breath, this heart-beat, this meager crust,
This joy, this sorrow, this hope, this lust,
This day, this week, this object of trust.

The next book, the next game, next triumph of will,
The next honor, next pay check, next valley or hill,
Next ecstatic moment, next moment that's still.

If there's any fixity, any abiding bliss,
It must be the next -- it isn't this.

TIDY RELIGION

Keep your religion tidy,
You wouldn't want to spoil it
-- Or do you worship that Jesus,
Who became this world's toilet?

James Howard Trott

WANTED POSTER

There is an old post-modern message
Posted at the Post Office:
An unwonted negation for political purposes:
"Wanted" says the poster,
But its object is not only unwanted,
But hated and feared.
Justice, that virtue so exalted it rates
A department of our government,
(Along with state, treasury, defense,
Interior and homeland security),
Is indeed served by the punishment of crime.
Before the lawyers and psychiatrists
Reinterpreted reality for us,
Crime was punished because it was crime.
Now it's for a deterrent, it's "corrections,"
It's all relative, depending on your relatives.
Some bright Machiavellian long ago
Discovered that crime could be guaranteed
Not to pay if its pursuit and punishment
Were adequately compensated.
Then "$10,000 for information
Leading to the apprehension . . ."
Made justice profitable -- which threatens to cancel
The older message preceding it: "Reward".
Which of the poster's promises do we trust?

Thistle Dew   Poems   Volume III

NO WASTED TIME

There is no wasted time --
No existential sump linked to a cosmic sewer
Which flows with the detritus
Of decaying years.
Every moment holds together in a whole,
Consists in Christ like every atom,
All vibrating, all vortical, vertical, veridical,
About his purposes
And good for the good for good.
There is no wasted time,
No wasted opportunity,
And no waste of lives.
Not even hell is a cesspool;
No bad cess, cesspool wasted.
There is no wasted time.

POSITION WIDE OPEN
(Based on two ads in the River Press)

There are few jobs you can be more certain to get
Than that one advertised in my hometown gazette:
"Fort Benton cemetery has . . . [personification -- pause]
An opening for a seasonal employee,"
-- Which seems unreasonable to me --
If the "opening" is the customary one,
Unless "seasonal" is some hopeful affirmation.

But on the same page (different column)
Is an ad that strikes me quite as solemn.
The same institution (the personable cem.)
Offers for sale a second hand item:
"One used, steel, overhead door."
Perhaps someone seasonal needs it no more.

BEING THERE

Being there,
The minimal spec,
The lowest requirement
For existence
And yet we
Grudgingly agree
Over time, being there
Is a respectable
Thing to be.
From family gatherings
To the incarnation,
Being there
Is counted participation.

BUCKS IN VELVET

Bucks in velvet cannot know
What hard-horned veterans they will be,
Though they're renewed in every age.
Their lost old antlers must seem
A loss indeed, not some presage,
Nor tender useless growths so green
As these their 'wildered heads adorn,
Known to them the crowns they are,
Badges and weapons: better horns.

CALVARY IS NOT OVER

The cross is no longer on a hill.
It is not outside the camp or wall.
Christ has been crucified
Once for all, but the sacrifice
Remains for all who will receive it.
There? -- Where?
Here, always;
Here and now.

NO CIVILIAN CASUALTIES

The Lord does not send armies when he invades a life.
He sends no heavy bombers, but experts with the knife.
Though he fights a full rebellion on a universal scale,
He takes the fortress bit but bit, kills none within the pale.
Though commanding angel legions, he dispatches just a few
To avoid civilian casualties as he conquers me or you.

A guerilla angel infiltrates disguised as a lingering doubt.
Watch out for sniper seraphs (there's always one about
Concealed in every landscape) to assassinate false pleasure;
Or a power or principality, silently sapping at your leisure,
Catching the enemy napping, taking captives one by one.
The casualties will turn out they who stuck to their own guns,
Who actively resist, despite generous offers of truce:
No casualty a civilian – and every prisoner turned loose.

DADDY

Daddy can't handle too much noise.
Daddy can't stand boys being boys —
Or girls being what girls will be.
He's too fragile – poor daddy.
Daddy can't handle disagreement,
Or the least dissent from what he says.
He needs respect, he needs to hear "yes,
Father, with your kind permission, sir."
When Daddy gets what he handles not,
He may go ballistic, run cold and hot,
He may grin grimly or he may frown,
But mostly Daddy just shuts down.
We have to protect him
He's our Achilles heel,
What Daddy can't handle
We all can feel.

GOD-DAMNED

There was never a God-damned counterfeit,
But began with a thing of gold;
Never a God-damned lie,
But where truth should have been told.

No man swears by a worm's name
Or its blood or throne or titles.
No -- men invoke blessed and cursed things,
In their God-damning recitals.
Humble yourself oh cursed man,
If aside the curse you'd toss,
To a God-damned Savior
On a God-damned cross.

FOOLIN' FISH

Foolin' fish is no life's work,
But when I feel the slack line jerk,
And see the flash of silver side,
Then foolin' fish is all my pride.

By narrow torrents, mountains blue
With worm or hopper, frontman true,
Or on broad currents, boat or waders,
Where singing fly tempts deep evaders –

It's foolin' fish that keeps heart green,
Makes body mend and mind serene --
Some things to remember, some to forget.
(And if at home, wife plans a meal
Without beef, pork, chicken or veal,
Trusting I can fool the fish,
Making but breading for that best dish --
Well, that's true love – and better yet!)

DUSK RIDERS

The cut fields lie still, gone of grain,
The swallows soar and dance and dart.
Higher the nighthawk cuts your heart,
With the pain of his winnowing.

FRUIT ON TREE

He put the fruit upon the tree,
The withered fig where sin had hanged,
The offered sweets that none could taste,
Except the one of purer race
Who fruit and image all had formed,
And cared to harvest more than husks:
He, tree, fruit, fee paid, last laborer there,
Took cursed fruit to paradise.

James   Howard   Trott

GIVE IT UP

Snakes nor rodents can regurgitate.
Their peristalsis is a one-way street
(Even when the snake swallows a rodent).

But we are blessed with the alimentary veto,
So why remain stubborn and finish a meal
We should never have begun --
That we could and should repeal?
Give it up!

GOD'S HINDER PART

I have seen little of God,
Little of his plan.
I have seen far too much,
Too much of man.

Why has he hidden
Me from his face?
Why always
Catch as catch can?

Stuck in a fissure,
Here as I'm bidden,
I think indeed I've glimpsed God's butt --
For man, oh man is elsewise what?

HEIRS OR ARTIFACTS

Heirs or artifacts,
Memorials of our days,
The secondary ends of every life
Born or made in phase. Secondary,
For the first of unregenerate hearts
Is self as heir or artifact
With which none parts,
Except through death-- or remaking.
In regeneration, heirs and artifacts
And self are left behind,
Cinders of the old creation.

IDEAS AND ARTIFACTS

Ideas are mental artifacts we collect and design,
Tailor-make for use as tools -- and weapons of mind
In a hostile world. But if this universe is
Ultimately hostile we will not overcome it like this --
And if it is not, perhaps we ought to rest,
Divest our minds and hands and set our artifacts aside.
They cannot save us. Nor can they abide.

James Howard Trott

JACKHAMMERS BEFORE EASTER

The jackhammers off and on all night
Maunday Thursday, Good Friday, and
Now, on Holy Saturday, too, threaten
To scourge and crucify sleep.

There is a gas leak they say, and
By irrevocable law, they must dig,
Must continue to search, must not
Stop until it's found and fixed.

My selfish soul wants to trivialize
"Father Forgive them for they
Know not what they do." --
But it was not mere incompetence he forgave.

My weak flesh longs for,
"It is finished," but he spoke not
Of a job delayed, but an eternal
Process concentrated in a moment --

"My God my God why hast thou forsaken. . ."
-- Not me, but Him, who took the
Jackhammers in his flesh, Maunday Thursday,
Good Friday and Holy Saturday.

And fixed the leak.

MARKING TIME

It's true that marking time is performing,
That nothing is accomplished and energy spent.
From a certain point of view it's hypocrisy,
Cowardice, putting off some inevitable.
Or, again, obliquely, it is the epitome of
The military expression, "hurry up and wait".
But hypocrisy blends into diplomacy,
Into courtesy and charity and faith,
Where marking time may be
A mildly active form of keeping the door --

MASONRY

There is a stone at the corner by which the rest are set
For plumb and square and level: a unique stone, and
 yet,
The rest are also stones -- in appearance much the same;
Like those at the other corners, also called by his name.

He is of our same matter, hewn to a perfect degree,
Yet quarried somewhere far away, beyond both sky and
 sea --
A foreign stone, a fellow stone, like and unlike all
 others;
A willing stone ground to mortar, to mortar a temple of
 brothers.

James Howard Trott

MT STANDS FOR . . .

MT stands for mountain.
Distant echoes peak to peak
Sound like those my empty heart
Can hear here every week.

There are no mountains here
Though every bus reads MT.
I suppose it means *mass transit*
But its singular to me.

The transport of your mountains
Thrust into sovereign sky —
That's the bus I've longed to take
As I live or as I die.

MT buses, empty hearts,
Empty mountain passes.
MT points to a higher home,
No place here surpasses.

MEMORIES MAY FADE

Memories fade away,
Blink out like lightening,
Thunderstruck bugs,
Flashes in the brain pan,

Like lives, names,
And nations,
But flowers fade, too,
Thus mark the beauty of an hour.
A flower of crystal or bronze
Is a book, but no blossom –
And no memory of a flower.

MISSING THE TRAIN

The train she runs on her own track,
On her own time, departs, and back,
Carries her own freight, passenger list,
Though I've been on the platform,
How often I missed
The train, I can't tell you. It's too hard,
To tell if she's on the line,
Or when she's in the yard,
When she's fueling up or dropping cars,
Whether off to Venus or back from Mars.
The train she runs on her own track,
I just listen for her clackety-clack.
Nothing else that I can do,
But listen for her WHOO-oh-WHOO!

James Howard Trott

THE MOUNTAIN

We see the mountain clearly
When we first think to ascend.
As further up and in we go
The less and less we seem to know.
'Til embraced by its pinnacles,
No benchmarks remain–
Yet in all ways all at once,
As the clouds clear,
Like alpine deer,
We see its whole domain.

TOO MANY FLOWERS
(after Mother Teresa)

There are too many minerals,
They stain the hills and plains,
Reacting always, tying up,
The precious gases of the air.

There are too many flowers --
The overcrowded hills and plains
Are being drained
Of all their precious minerals.

There are too many children,
The overcrowded hills and plains
Are being stripped of all
Their minerals, flowers and mice.

These are so many vermin.
No doubt the basic problem is
There aren't enough
Bloody-taloned owls.

NATIVE GRASS

The native grass flickers
In green gray blazes.
The roadside mustard
Stands and bows.
The winter wheat
Beyond the road
Runs green with surf
Like exotic seas,
And on the further hills
The spring crops curl
With patterned combs
That flow stretching
Across their breadth.
There is no pattern
To be seen among them –
Each appears driven
By its own force,
Though we know
It is all one wind.

James Howard Trott

NAUTICAL DISASTER

The steersman was asleep,
The owner on board,
The captain stayed with the ship
Under the storm of his own wrath,
The disaster and its rescue.
And though I called him
Out of fear,
And for all the wrong reasons,
He heard and answered,
Rebuked my heart,
And calmed the wind and wave.

ONE LEAF

In the aspen amphitheatre,
The sound of one leaf trembling
Becomes a roar of applause
For the wind's music.

PSEUDOMORPH

In minerology, something taking the
form of something other...
...
Forms of fossils, crystal shapes,
Of materials not truly this or that :
False forms, but nevertheless,
Reminders and memorials
To what truly was...
Perhaps is... still somewhere else
Real.

ROADSIDE MEMORIALS
(Montana)

So few, so precious the people
On these prairies,
That we raise up reminders
For every wreck on every road;
Reckoning as persons still
Our inefficient dead.

SELF-PROTECTION

Since the first conscious reflex of self-protective sin,
We know the move, the instinctive spin, of accusing others
Of what we've done – not merely denying, "I'm not the one,"
But pointing a finger and describing the deed, as
Of some other, in our desperate need to cover self.
Thus tyrants arrest, accuse their leading opponents
Who refuse to conform or submit to their regimes
And charge these innocent with their own evil schemes.

To defeat this maneuver one may accumulate peculiar,
Syntheses of truth and power and opportune justice,
As on very few occasions exploited by rare visionaries,
Or parrying the corrupt cop as only one innocent ever could,
Who stood accusing and damning himself before his accuser:
Self-protection turned inside out. -- Who was the loser?

YOU SEND A BOY

In an age when competence is *de rigueur*, by the
 numbers,
Every boy's enrolled in school, taught the trade of sure:
Put on a sports team, one position played, each, every;
A long apprentice, kept to his articles, bound
To do his homework until a man is found,
Since only then his can-do can be respected, his calling
Agreed upon and he be sent, hitherto but exercise and
 pretence.
But you! You always send a boy! You make
 incompetence
Your chief criterion – whether to lead, or debate
 opponents,
Or fight them; to receive your instructions or to judge:
So many are the cases, they mumble like a mob.
-- Why send <u>me</u> to do a man's job?

SPRING FROST

The magnolia mourns its bitter blight in brown petal
 tears.
Those sprang first in joy last week in response to
 spring's
Own promise, the assurance of what seemed freely
 offered,
Warmly given, now in harshest cold withdrawn.

James Howard Trott

I have a list on crisp brown pages, long since rosen,
A list of hopeful blossoms begun, since found frozen,
That flutter daily, dully to the worm-rich ground --
Among them few full-swollen blooms may be found.

In the same lot, not far from the mourning-coloured
     tree,
The bare-limbed shriven Rose of Sharon shivers
     lifelessly,
Longtime stays dead almost to the summer solstice.
No sign of joy in it, no heaven-hued spring-time bower;
Its limbs embrace not spring, but hold on to suffering,
Hold it closer than hope before erupting into long-lived
     flower.

THE SWEETEST FRAME
"I dare not trust the sweetest frame..." - hymn

    Whether of flesh or brick and stone;
    Of finest fabric, or of gold alone;
    Of beautiful images, beautiful thoughts,
    Perfect logic, or bonniest mots --
    I dare to trust no frame less sweet
    Than His who gathers, will complete the whole --
    Who worked until himself diminished,
    On an ugly frame, could say, "It's finished."

TOWER IN THE FOG

Jesus is the tumbled tower, the silo of Siloam,
That fell for errors in the other stones.
Jesus is the beacon beam lost in fog,
Where sad ships roam;
The lighthouse that toppled before the storm.

Jesus is the rain that never reached the ground,
Sucked up in the desert, returned to the clouds.

Jesus is the mystery in every marriage,
The unaccountable tall brightness
In the low-down dim.

TOO MUCH

"This is too much," I said,
Meaning 'more than I could wish for;'
Then, "This is too much,"
Meaning 'I wish for a great deal more.'

James Howard Trott

WEDDING JEWELRY

Every word a silver coin,
Every sentence a sum,
Every metaphor fines to gold
In every poem to which they come:
A diamond, faceted every way
For a dowry treasured
'Til the wedding day.

WINTER ROSES

Swaying in the harsh winds of January
The dawn rose stalks are covered with blooms,
Warm burdens of tender petals,
Newly colorless, gray, against the white snow,
Except for the brilliant red,
The cardinal huddled briefly
Among the sparrows.

THE WATER IS WIDE (as per Dylan)

The water is wide, the lakes are great,
No matter what you think of love, or hate --
Much to overcome, a long way to go;
Brothers let's get aboard and let's all row.

JESUS' IDOLATRY

Thou shalt not make unto thee any graven image,
No god in likeness of created thing --
Thus Moses, the law.
The reverberations have not ended nor will
Until this sphere's forever still.

The prophets warned Israel where idols would lead:
The conformity of idolaters to the image they made:
Unable to talk, or think, hear or see; to die:
Poetic justice for wrong homage paid.

But some corner was turned, in one idolatry,
An arcane form in Cana of Galilee,
When God made himself in the image of man,
And seems to have worshipped
The work of his hands.

"Idol worship!" you, say. What else call it
When someone acts in inordinate love for another,
Made as important to him as God?
Dies for his handiwork, calling it "brother!"

There's but one thing keeps Jesus from the charge,
Though he loved lesser, abandoned greater:
To an image of his own hands, sacrificed self.
It was image not of creature, but of Creator.

This one exception to the prohibition is my song:
As I, poor image, gaze this sacrifice upon,
Scales fall from my idol eyes, the metamorphosis is
    mine,
I become like the Idolater whose sacrifice is divine.

BY ANIMADVERSION

Lord, so much of my motive to do
Is to do the lesser, to escape you
And your calling to the higher and harder,
The best of your treasure, rarest in your larder.
I am driven down by my own heart's fear
And the doubt significance will ever appear.
But if the true is universal, the universal true,
Who stands and waits serves you, too,
And may have mail for those who come.

Now no horse hooves or train rails hum:
Electronic pulses through air and wire
Are hyperactive with this one desire,
To do nothing frantically with latest tech,
Taking the old joke to its ultimate wreck:
"One may gain th'experience of fifty years,
While others shed fifty-times one-year's tears."

Yet what rhymes and what is true,
And what worth knowing or doing, you
Alone can demonstrate, often through negation.
Give me grace Lord, and new animation.

AS ON A SHORE

Thou and I as on a shore
Have rushed the thousands on before
And thought it good. But see how
Many other waves now further go
And how the pioneers on pour
As but a line of foam, and how
They now at last recede as I and thou.

THE MEAL AFTER THE BATTLE

For three years the Devil set his gang
To ambush Jesus at every other turn.
Last nail driven, the Gangster still mocked,
But God himself put on the real burn
Of hell, the ever-beating we deserved.
Satan and the world were small-time there
Before the One Jesus truly served --
Whom He feared, and who could truly tempt.
He alone drove him to the mat.
That was trial, trial by combat
Waged for the wager of your soul and mine.

None sits down to eat
When he's come from defeat.
The victors feast when battle is done.
The meal belongs to the One who won.

James Howard Trott

BLUE MOUNTAIN

I can't, I said, you know I can't, I've got to finish school.
OK, he said, -- your choice, guess I'd be a fool
To say it mattered, it's my fault, too -- I'll do the cost
    accountin'.
They make it quick and easy -- up on Blue Mountain.

Up on Blue Mountain they give you back your life,
The one you thought that you deserved, they do it with
    a knife.
And don't blame Blue Mountain if what you take away,
Wasn't what you gambled for -- Blue Mountain didn't
    say.

He was better than a lot, he stuck. A few years after,
We married with our degrees, knew some kinds of
    laughter,
But after fifteen years of hearing only phantom voices,
We knew Blue Mountain gave us more than choices.

In the winter I see snow up on Blue Mountain,
In the springtime I see green up on Blue Mountain,
And most all the year around, winds toss the pines,
On that loneliest of places, where the lost sun shines.

BODY AS DOG

The body is like a dog – you can't let it out
Into the backyard without keeping an eye on it.
You can't take it for a walk without its leash.
It may embarrass you acutely in public settings.

And yet we dog lovers would never be without one.
A dog is both a source of joy and a helper,
From pulling sleds to guarding the front door.
(The body is not a wolf – though there's wildness in
   the flesh.)

Jesus wanted a dog so much, he left heaven to get
   one.
And when it was mistreated by his friends,
When we all thought he'd lost it, he insisted
The Holy Spirit go, retrieve it from the pound.

CIRCULARITY

To facet a stone
First make it a cabochon.
To make it perfectly round –
First facets should be ground.

James Howard Trott

COMMUNICATION

Aside from the fact the crowd's not hushed
(There is no crowd, there is no tent)
Every communication or attempt
Is a trapeze act – it takes at least two.
Both must reach, with timing true.
One may swing from a far platform,
The other releases from bar or grasp,
But in the end they both must clasp
Each other's hand – or the no-crowd's gasp
Will be at yet another fall.
There's no tent, neither net at all.

MY COMPLAINT

Not that he's malevolent,
Nor that he doesn't care.
Not that he's absent-minded,
With wildly-unkempt hair;
But that he's incompetent,
Just can't keep track.
That's the shape my unbelief
Keeps taking back.

CROSS – GRAIN

It's hard to work cross-grain,
To plane, to sand, to finish clean.
It's hard to live in world of sin,
Where every day that we begin
Is begun against the tides and winds,
Inclinations and institutions,
The philosophies, tenets, indeed the vows
Of seeming millions, across our bows.

The clean lumber God made,
Still lies beneath our hand and blade.
The accidents of storm and sin,
Can not deflect what we begin,
Where we discern, shape, go
With grain and current. This know.

FLAG IN RAIN

Now we fly the flag in rain
No longer humble . . .

The respect to it we once thought due
And bowing to weather . . .

No flag, no fealty, no rule, no reign
Falls upon us . . .

James Howard Trott

THE FLAVOR OF MORTALITY

The flavor of mortality
These days
Is a metallic taste,
Unpleasant in all ways.
No savor of sweet,
Of salt or sour,
Not even sharp bitter,
But dull in its power
To hurry all I do
A half step too fast:
This tincture in each dish --
That may be my last.

JOY IN THIS FLESH

We know not which shall pass direct,
While yet the other doth perfect
His - Her - love toward the greater -
To see it then a little later.
Yet this we have, do passion know,
Need not that lose to greatest show,
For as I in your flesh can see
Such joy, so in this flesh of ours must he.

THE FRACTILE

Both infinite and infinitesimal,
God's grace is both greater and more delicate,
Spirals down so — for our eyes too small,
And looms large, for our minds too great.
The fractile – order out of chaos -- too,
Sings of it: nothing's random, nothing old – or new,
No scale of reference but what refers to you.

MOULTING GEESE

It is no coincidence
The grown geese moult
When their goslings
Are young and vulnerable.

The Lord clips their wings
So they can not take to air,
Leave responsibility
And those for whom they care.

Loves he not our children
More than these?

James   Howard   Trott

GIVING GIFTS

Giving gifts is fraught with fractious
Thoughts and faultlines
Run between the shifts of care,
Exasperation,
Split of favor, favoritism.
Giving gifts is never easy,
Costs are chalked up many columned.
Why give gifts, make sacrifice?
No one's ever pleased with these,
Or not for long.
It seems that giving gifts is primal –
Something we have got from God.

HEAD IN THE CLOUDS

A lovely city with its head in the clouds
Across the ripples the boat houses row,
As our Christmas daughter flies back to Uganda.
Lights high and misty, lights low and breaking
Light small and going, into the distance.
A lovely city -- growing so
With its head in the clouds.

GOD AT HIS MOST PATHETIC

I am an American after all, and a male,
Therefore I fail to find it plausible,
Still pause and mill afresh the news
That God this flesh did choose and wept.
Had he kept a stiffer upper stoic, bore up
Through his rough patch (naturally I admit
He had to endure an extreme or two)
With more solemnity I'd easier believe.

The trombone of his last troubles blared,
The tenor of his voice cried pitifully what?
How could the sacred have sounded scared?
Poor tune played on the harp of God's gut?
At his most pathetic God whimpered at sin.
Don't suppose his groans will drag me in!

HIGH WORK

The solo sailor and the solo flyer
Are journeyers alone, further and higher
Than human friend can go.
That is indeed the end
To which they go:
To self to show,
And to credentialed be below.

James Howard Trott

But solo flight and voyage far
Are finite, run against the bar
Of human limits, which ever call
The lonely back to all and all.
And even when human friend is shunned,
Ground and shore wait, solos done.

The man who flies above the clouds
Or he who works atop the roofs
Of human houses knows
He only lives as one of those
Who ever stays aware, as proof he strays
In high and alien paths, his days
There numbered, holy and haloed,
And liable to a sudden end
Should he exist solely.
The pilot and the roofer know
They are of the earth which lies below.
To earth they will return --
And yet, this alien height seems ultimate.

IDIOT SAVANT

Among the mysteries that are men
Those clearly disabled much portend:
The blind, the deaf, the sick, the lame
Give our hearts' ills clearer name.
Genius, too, and consummate skill

Teach us amidst so much else ill,
That excellence in body, in soul, in mind
Were our first state – again to find.
But best mentors, those best able
To show us our state in a world post-Babel
Are they who exhibit both weal and wants,
And are sometimes labelled "idiot-savants".
Incapable of many basic tasks,
Yet solving conundrums as though the masks
Of drama dual, were worn by one actor,
Both wiseman and fool.
And so you are and so am I
Disabled, unable to live and die
Alone – and yet with God and friend,
Best and worst share to the end.

IN STARS AND INSTARS

Astrologers in our age without superstitions
Calculate much more than the stars' positions,
They know their substance
And their histories --
Ah, for them there are no mysteries left.

Bereft of any great nebulae of unknowing,
We who are from tele- to micro-scope going,
Will find confusing,

And perhaps amusing
Among insects more stars to glimpse.

For nymphs, larvae and even some adults
Evolve each toward their final results,
Where Darwin and Freud
See them properly employed,
That is, mating maturity.

But the obscurity I was headed for before sex,
Interposed, (always some complex or another),
Was that insect "instars," ages
Are the various stages
Through which they preach their sermons.

For what determines what, who studies whom,
Seem to me unclear. Ponder this doom:
Why should the ends of entomology
Not be combined with astrology?

KEYOTIC

Perhaps all this indicating life's chaotic
Is a sign my soul needs some antibiotic.
God loves a fool, his will is exotic –
Life without a "key" – but rather <u>quix</u>otic.

THE LAST ONE KISSED

Life accumulates until we grow --
How to be last kissed I now know.
Two lessons I remember – remember and blush
About being last kissed, about the rush –
Of feeling, a kind of greed,
A sense of desiring, of want, of need.
The first was among religious youth
Already cynical about presumed truth,
A game "choo choo" and I the novice
Ready to be baptized like the troops of Clovis,
And while all the rest indeed were kissed –
When I puckered up for my moment of bliss,
I was slapped, the conventional end.
(I remember the sorrowful face of one friend.)
The second time, kinswoman of my wife,
An actress, dazzling, met in real life
(Or perhaps in a moment of greater confusion,
Fresh from her play, still wearing illusion).
All the rest, blood kin, she heartily kissed,
And I, the last, would not have missed!
But to me she offered a hearty hand,
And deeply chagrinned, I felt unmanned,
Unmannerly, bumptious, and rude
For what I had wanted -- thus we delude
Ourselves and think to presume
The best embraces when occasions loom.
But through only such slaps and denials
Do we grow to know the love in our trials
And learn to wait for what we miss
Which will surely at last -- be the very best kiss.

James   Howard   Trott

MY LOVER AND I

When my lover sighs and I,
Sighs there are in heaven.

When my lover and I see,
Visions then of heaven.

When my lover and I touch,
Heaven comes to earth.

When my lover and I pray,
Ecstasy in heaven all day.

MAGNITUDE

It is a big country
With a big sky.
Man's mark is small upon it –
So big spaces sigh
Or signal with purer signs.
And big storms echo it,
Against the lines of mountains,
Still, distant, high.

Man is small upon it
And inclined to act small:
To grow grim in his struggles,

To expect nothing at all,
To hide his head in a bottle
To resist the great call.

Nonetheless it's a big place,
Immensity written large,
And demands a kind of fealty
To what or whom is in charge.

So some learn the human part
Of magnitude, bigness of heart.

WHEN FIRST WE FLEW
(On a hatch of Mayfly subimagoes)

These insubstantial ugly ones –
Subimagoes, are called "duns"
By the fishermen who flock
To their swarming hatches,
Knowing the fish are drawn, too,
Hungry for catches.

Clammy-bodied, soft and dull,
At your sudden advent, you feeble race.
You come in waves, pile about lights –
Your insect mind filling brief time and place.
Immature creatures much like you,
We failed no doubt, when first we flew.

James   Howard   Trott

MINIATURE HANDPRINTS

There are miniature handprints
On the mirror in our room
Only three feet from the floor.
I see them in the bloom
Of the morning sun – smeary,
Besmirching its perfections,
But making happier, clearer reflections.

MOTHER MOUNTAIN

The Everests and Matterhorns
Do not hate, though thought inimical.
They stand surrounded by frozen glory,
By destroying winds and steeps and heights.
They conquer not because they care,
But because they are, they're there.

The mothers of this world
Love always and in finite detail,
From the grubbiest item of infant laundry
To the greatest acts of betrayal or crime,
They cannot be made not to care,
For that is what they are.

God is a mountain and a mother,
He stands, he cares, he is.

Thistle Dew   Poems   Volume III

MARCH TREE

   The blood red
   Black cherry blossoms
   Bow white before the blue.

THE NAPOLEON OF BASKETBALL

     Able saw I
     Ere I was elbowed.

KNICKKNACK (URNED INCOME)

   You who value knickknacks
      above all else,
   And worship those
     upon your shelf,
   Are doomed to stand
     on the mantle
       yourself.

James Howard Trott

NOT QUITE

I was "not quite" from birth on,
Day and night,
Not quite ready, not quite prepared,
Not quite on time,
Not quite bright or strong or quick or tough.
But some strange sight
Of that which was enough
Has made me all right.
Despite "not quite"--

GOD GIVE US METAPHORS

God give us metaphors,
We vary so . . .
We are so dull
So wary to go
About our learning
And our living –
Show us parables
And with your giving,
Give us Thine Spirit
To enliven the eyes
Of stone-blind hearts,
To syllogize,
To interpret, to see.
Be thou our metaphor –
To show us Thee.

PACE for the RACE

The pace of poetry is the pace of being.
The race of the poet is the race of man.
The pace of the race is beyond any seeing,
But poetry's pace is the pace of being.

A PARABOWL

And she said...
"That small white throne you're hugging now
Is a sign of things to come.
You hold it in misery for stupid things you done,

"But a great white throne is coming, boy,
You'll bow before it, too,
Repent your ways and get God's help
Or you know what he'll do...

"He'll ... flush that john like you flushin' this,
And see you as you see that stuff
You're chucking up, sure enough!
But someone took your place if you ask him to.

"There's life indeed not misery and despair.
That throne can be a sign of hope,
Jesus already bowed down there.

James Howard Trott

"The sins he choked out weren't his own,
The cup he drank was mine,
The judgment filled him up with dregs,
Of sacrificial wine.

"He took full measure of the hell
His children would have received,
And said, 'It's finished' for each and all
Who says, 'Yes, I believe.'

"So let go your throne, let go the liquor,
Grab hold of Jesus, before you get sicker."

PHILLATTITUDE

Philly is a funky town – I love it
For attitude it takes the crown – I love it.
It sneers and brags
And rolls and rags,
It drinks its joys
From paper bags –
I love it.

RAINBOW EAST RAINBOW WEST

Last evening after we had flown the continent,
And navigated our way through loved ones,
We settled in the empty farmhouse,
Which is our mute ally in looking north.
But when the unpredicted thunderstorm
Came up out of the southwest,
We had our secret smugness
Reinforced and diminished
(We tell them every year it is
We who bring the rain)
By a rainbow in the east at its passing.
Such a rainbow I do not recall --
A whole bow so low to the earth,
So small an arc in such a local sky.
The colors were intense.
Thus it was excess at morning dawn,
When Thunder sounded the southwest again,
A storm preceded by a golden outrider,
Misty cloud at its center, lit by focused beam
Of rising sun, and above it arching,
Another rainbow, partial and high.
The northern half found no ground,
In the sharp clear skies that side of downpour.
The mist and the storm sailed the south eastward,
Leaving a tiny remnant of the bow.
Rainbows East, Rainbows West,
Promises for every traveller's quest.

James Howard Trott

ROBBING PETER

In the church there is no
"Robbing Peter to pay Paul" –
For God possesses
And provides for all.

Paul knows this,
Therefore needs to apply
To the source for all
His rewards and supply,

While sometimes Peter
Will find it his job
To forestall those
Who might otherwise rob.

SATELLITE

Sent into orbit before your time,
Cape Canaveral has lost your sign.
Broken transmissions,
Bits of thoughts
From a docking station
For cosmonauts.
Girl, there's a God
Who loves you.

Thistle Dew   Poems   Volume III

SEA FERVOR

I must go down to the loo again,
To the lonely loo on the lea,
And all I ask is some oakum
And a fairly smooth stretch of sea –
Where the thunder claps
As the wave slaps,
And the crests may tickle your fancy --
Oh I must go down to the loo again,
I tell you I'm feeling antsy.

I must go down to the loo again,
To the lonely loo on the lea,
Yes, I know it was only an hour ago,
But I feel it most desperately.
I'm feeling crook,
And I fear old cook
Put bilgewater in the tea.
I need to go down to the loo again –
All the forecastle doth agree.

I want to go down to the loo again,
To the lonely loo on the lea,
Where the winch's creak
Serenades the reek,
As a man unburdened may be.
Where the slap of the top
And the scuppers slop
Are drowned out most merrily.
Oh I must go down to the loo again,
Though its tardy I may be.

James Howard Trott

I must go down to the loo again,
To the lonely loo on the lea.
Though the scene be rude,
There is solitude
Such as seldom sailors see.
This one doubt I reck:
Why the aft-roof deck
On ships whether frigate or sloop
Though never ever defaced thereby
Is always called the poop?

SKY BLUE PINK

Sky blue pink
No matter what you think --
No matter what your theory,
How you talk yourself weary --
I'm just glad
My old Dad
Taught me sky blue pink.
Much is not as it seems.
Sometimes a dream
Turns out closer
To the way things are,
Like a thunderstorm or star
Or a Montana sunset
While your systems run
Down the cosmic sink --
The universe the color
Of Sky Blue Pink.

THE SMELL OF MORNING

There is a smell of morning . . .
Like the smell of first thaw . . .
A still moment of rest . . .
And another moment of fierce drama
--Smell of storm – its breaking
--Thunder crash, like mountains upthrust
Or earthquake cataclysm,
Which "Grand Canyon Suite"
Echoes as from the wall
In the dramatic trumpet's call --
Which Disney transforms
With a daring and sudden shot
Moving out over the Canyon Rim.
But the visual drama is not quite
Equivalent to the music's sound,
Nor either to things and smells.
And words cannot reach as deep,
Yet reach further than any of these.

STONE OVEN

Jesus refused to turn stones into bread,
But he turned bread into more bread;
Turned living bread into broken bread;
Fed broken bread into living stones.

James Howard Trott

STYLE

Every place, each time and gender
Has its style of big pretender:

Designer brands of nonchalance,
Decorated fragile fronts.

Generations may vary,
Stages, ages, always wary.

Yet open, easy, fearless air
Turns out the same most anywhere.

SUDDEN GHOST

See! In the mirror!
What ghost doth appear!
Is it Marley reminding
Of rites of remorse?
Nay, that squinch-eyed phantom
Wants remorse nor ransom –
It is only yourself,
Just short of a corpse!

SWEET AND CARELESS

Sweet and careless, sweet and uncaring,
Is any other as hard for bearing?

Smiles and soft words, hands warmly shaken –
Give me the grouch (whose word is worth taking)

"I didn't mean it," "I'm really sorry" – –
More worthless words
You can't beg, buy, or borry.

TOP RUNG POETRY

I have a friend stood up on the top rung of a ladder.
Life-changing it was, and though the Yankee and
Victorian in me would first prefer an ominous moral,
His life was not changed for the worse –
So I conclude straight analogy is not enough.
Sometimes it's good to stand on the top rung of a
      ladder.
He did indeed fall – and it was a thirty-two footer,
Fully extended – and he fully extended, too,
So his head began nearly thirty-four feet up.
(Don't go all modern and analytic: there's things
You do not know -- outside the box -- such as
The ratio of nominal to actual height in extension
      ladders.)

James Howard Trott

A driveway offered its unreceptive surface for his
    landing.
He fell to the shattering of many bones.
(I suppose I'm not the only one working on ladders
Who occasionally takes sightings of where he might
    land,
But usually there's no choice, the job dictates the
    substratum.)
The allegory occurs to one, but it's not enough either:
I know a man descended from the top rung of a ladder,
Fell and shattered himself upon the resistant globe –
Even then not enough to convict or convince,
But that the doctors told him he'd be paralyzed;
That he'd never walk, and that he'd never work;
That he did rise up to walk and work -- and out of it all
(Not just anagogy, although that, too, seems
    inescapable)
He came to Christ – literally and with joy.

TREES IN MY FRONT YARD

    The ancient oak in my west, front yard
    Is a more essential tree
    Than any I knew where planted I grew
    At home in the west,
    With the west at home in me.

The woods of this fair place and clime
Are woods indeed in spring and fall,
Not prairies blown about by the wind
In the windy west,
Where the west was at home in me.

Ah, Lord, the trees in my front yard,
Are yours, and you are at home I see
At sunset. Here I can offer once again
The treeless west,
To the yew between the west and me.

WAR OF THE WARNINGS
(In memory of the great capitalist Adam Smith)

Every notice warns you twice.
Both require you to be nice —
First, to your conscience,
Then to the mighty buck.
Try and heed both.
Oh, yes -- good luck!

James Howard Trott

Other books by James Howard Trott include:

Immanence : Selected, Collected Poems, Volume One, 1967-1988. James Howard Trott. copyright 2003/2010. Available 2015 at Createspace eBookstore, etcetera

Contingency: Selected, Collected Poems, Volume Two 1989-2001. James Howard Trott. copyright 2015. Available at Createspace eBookstore and other online sources

Land, Light, Wind, and Water: Prairie Quartet. First edition published privately, in Philadelphia, copyright 1993 James Howard Trott. James Edwards Trott, editor. Revised Edition, copyright 2009, 2015 Available at Createspace eBookstore and other online sources.

Conceptions and images : Pro-life poems with Prisoners' Pardons (orig editions 1992.1993 and 1998) Revised. James Howard Trott. Available 2015 at Createspace eBookstore and other online sources.

A Sacrifice of Praise: An Anthology of Christian Poetry in English from Caedmon to the mid-Twentieth Century. Second Edition – Nashville: Cumberland House, 2006.

A Gallows Set Upon a Hill: An Historical Novel (about the Salem Witch Trials) James Howard Trott copyright 2002/2015. Available 2015 at Createspace eBookstore and other online sources.

Trott All Day: A Compendium:Trotts Through The Ages. James Howard Trott. Copyright 2004, 2015 Available 2015 at Createspace eBookstore and other online sources.

Was That Thunder: A Memoir Of Pro-life Rescue, 1988-1997. James H. Trott. Copyright 2007/2015. Available 2015 at Createspace eBookstore and other online sources.

Thistle Dew   Poems   Volume III

James Howard Trott

www.ingramcontent.com/pod-product-compliance
Lightning Source LLC
Chambersburg PA
CBHW020004050426
42450CB00005B/301